". . . when I'm dead 25 years, people are going to begin to recognize me."

— ATTRIBUTED TO SCOTT JOPLIN

Scott Joplin
The King of Ragtime

By C. Ogbu Sabir

GRAPHIC DESIGN
Robert E. Bonaker / Graphic Design & Consulting Co.

PROJECT COORDINATOR
James R. Rothaus / James R. Rothaus & Associates

EDITORIAL DIRECTION
Elizabeth Sirimarco Budd

COVER PHOTO
Portrait of Scott Joplin
©Archive Photos

Library of Congress Cataloging-in-Publication Data
Sabir, C. Ogbu.
Scott Joplin : the king of ragtime / by C. Ogbu Sabir.
p. cm.
Includes bibliographical references and index.
Summary: Examines the life and accomplishments of the well-
known ragtime pianist and composer, who wrote over 500
pieces of music, including a ballet and two operas.
ISBN 1-56766-746-5 (library reinforced : alk. paper)

1. Joplin, Scott, 1868–1917 — Juvenile literature.
2. Composers — United States — Biography — Juvenile
literature. [1. Joplin, Scott, 1868–1917. 2. Composers.
3. Afro-Americans — Biography.] I. Title.

ML3930.J66 S23 2000
780'.92 — dc21   00-023697
[B]

Contents

The Entertainer

After the American Civil War, life in the United States slowly began to return to normal. Businesses began to do well again. Railroads moved more and more people to the Midwest and the West. Cowboys and railroad workers enjoyed relaxing in the evenings, often by listening to music at **saloons.** During the mid-1880s, the piano was by far the most popular instrument. Piano players, both black and white, could make good money from their salary and tips.

Scott Joplin was one of these musicians. This quiet, well-dressed, dark-skinned black man played **ragtime** music at the Maple Leaf Club in Missouri. Joplin drew crowds of people who danced, sang, and tapped their feet to the beat as he played the piano. Because of Joplin's way of playing **melodious** tunes with an upbeat **tempo,** the Maple Leaf Club had become the most popular place to hear ragtime. His music made people feel good. People came from all around to hear this music. Joplin was soon known to locals as "The Entertainer."

Scott Joplin was born in eastern Texas, about three years after the Civil War. He was born in 1867 or 1868, but no one is sure of the exact date. Scott's father, Giles, was born a slave around 1842 in the South. He became free in the 1850s. Scott's mother, Florence Givens, was **freeborn** around 1841 in Kentucky. Scott was the second child born to Giles and Florence Joplin. He had an older brother, two younger sisters, and two younger brothers.

©Bettmann/CORBIS

SCOTT JOPLIN LED THE AFRICAN AMERICAN
MUSICIANS WHO CREATED A NEW KIND OF
MUSIC CALLED RAGTIME.

SHARECROPPERS LIKE THE JOPLINS WORKED THE LAND OWNED BY WHITE FARMERS. THEY RECEIVED VERY LITTLE PAY OR A PORTION OF THE CROPS IN RETURN FOR THEIR HARD WORK.

The Joplins worked as **sharecroppers** in eastern Texas. African American sharecroppers worked picking crops for white farmers. The sharecroppers did not own the land and were paid very little for working long, hard hours. The Joplins moved several times, trying to find a better life. When Scott was a very young boy, his father heard that the railroad was hiring men. They moved to a town called Texarkana, located on the Texas-Arkansas border. Scott's father moved his family there in search of a better job and a steady income.

After his father found a job as a railroad worker, the Joplins were able to rent a small house in a part of town where other black people lived. It was in this neighborhood that Scott grew up and began his lifelong pursuit of a career in music.

The Joplins were a musical family. Scott's mother played the banjo and sang, and his father played the fiddle. Some people say that Scott's father played in a plantation orchestra. The band played at dances and parties that the slave masters held.

By the age of seven, Scott played both the fiddle and the banjo — but he was most interested in playing the piano. The Joplins did not own a piano. It is thought that Scott was allowed to play at the home of a white attorney while his mother cleaned the man's house.

Soon everyone could see that Scott had a special talent. Several music teachers in the black community offered to teach him for no charge because he was such a fast learner. They enjoyed working with a student who was so talented.

A teacher named J. C. Johnson was especially important to Scott. Johnson was part African American and part Native American. Johnson may have taught Scott how to read music. This was an important achievement. Many blacks at the time only knew how to play music by hearing it and then repeating the sounds. This is called playing music "by ear." Johnson also taught Scott about European **classical music.**

Later, a German-born musician named Julius Weiss taught Scott. Hearing of the young boy's talents, he also taught him for free. Weiss is credited with developing Scott's understanding of European classical music. This would have a long-lasting effect on Scott's musical interests. Scott's love of the **opera** probably began during this time.

Scott was a quiet and serious student. He loved music and wanted to devote his time and energy to it. His father did not believe that a black man could make a good living by playing music. He did not want to encourage his son's musical ability. Scott's mother felt differently. She helped him in any way she could. Scott's parents often argued about his future.

By age 11, Scott could read music. He also played several instruments well. Most important of all, he could **compose** music. He often made up his own tunes or improved those written by others. It was about this time that Scott's father left his family. His mother then had to support the children. She worked as a maid in the home of white families. This job did not pay very much. After about two years, around 1881 or 1882, Scott's mother finally was able to buy a piano for him. Scott would do chores for neighbors to earn money. Then he would buy sheet music to play on the piano, spending five or ten cents on each piece.

When Scott was 16 years old, he formed the Texas Medley **Quartette** with two friends and his brothers, Robert and Will. (Although a quartette usually has four members, they had five.) Scott sang with the group, but people often asked him to perform alone, too. He played piano at many events and parties. Scott became well known as a talented musician throughout his community.

In his late teens or early 20s, Scott decided to leave home. He set out on his own to have a career in music. Scott was determined to be a successful musician. During this era, black men had few career choices. They were usually farmers, laborers, or servants. Scott felt that being a musician was a respectable career of which he could be proud.

©Library of Congress

DURING THE TIME OF SLAVERY, MUSIC AND DANCE WERE IMPORTANT TO AFRICAN AMERICANS. IT WAS THE ONLY PART OF THEIR CULTURE THAT MOST SLAVES HAD BEEN ABLE TO BRING WITH THEM FROM AFRICA. OVER THE YEARS, AFRICAN AMERICANS HAVE CREATED MANY EXCITING FORMS OF MUSIC. THEY ARE RESPONSIBLE FOR THE BIRTH OF RAGTIME, JAZZ, THE BLUES, ROCK-AND-ROLL, AND RAP.

Ragtime

Piano players were popular during the late 1880s. Scott had no trouble finding jobs. He played his music at many different places, including fairs, restaurants, stores, theaters, dance halls, and saloons. He traveled around the Midwest, living for a while in Sedalia, Missouri.

In 1890, Scott moved to St. Louis, Missouri. There he worked at the Silver Dollar Saloon. A black pianist named John Turpin was a barkeeper there. One of Turpin's sons, Tom, was to become one of Scott's longtime friends. The two of them were **aspiring** musicians. They were both pianists and composers. Tom Turpin was the first composer to have his ragtime sheet music published.

African American slaves had brought their music with them to America. They passed these African musical traditions on to their children and grandchildren.

In the 1890s, musicians such as Scott Joplin began to mix the beat and rhythms of African-inspired music with European American music. The combination of the two was melodious, but many people thought it sounded somewhat "ragged." It seemed as if the beat of the music had "ragged time." This is how the music became known as ragtime.

Ragtime is happy and uplifting music. It can be played on many different instruments but is usually played on the piano. Ragtime piano players use the left hand to play a steady, regular beat that is similar to a march. The right hand plays the melody. The melody is fast and irregular compared with the regular beat played by the left hand.

©Missourie Historical Society

SALOONS LIKE THE OLD ROCK HOUSE
IN ST. LOUIS WERE POPULAR PLACES FOR
PEOPLE TO GATHER, LISTEN TO MUSIC,
AND ENJOY FOOD AND DRINK.

©Missouri Historical Society

W. C. HANDY (AT THE PIANO) WAS ANOTHER POPULAR MUSICIAN IN THE SALOONS OF ST. LOUIS. JUST AS JOPLIN IS THE "KING OF RAGTIME," HANDY IS THE "FATHER OF THE BLUES." LIKE JOPLIN, HANDY HELPED MORE PEOPLE APPRECIATE AFRICAN AMERICAN MUSIC.

Ragtime music was unusual in its day and quite difficult to play. It was also difficult to write on sheet music, which musicians use to learn and play music. As ragtime's popularity grew, composers wrote simple songs so that less skillful musicians could play them. Although Joplin never made his songs easier to play, his music remained popular.

Ragtime often was played in saloons. For many years, it was considered to be low-class music. Sometimes ragtime music was **instrumental,** but many songs had **lyrics.** The lyrics were sometimes **vulgar** or insulting to blacks. Although ragtime was associated with blacks, many blacks did not like it. They thought that the words showed blacks in an unkind light.

Joplin was determined to make ragtime music more popular. He felt that ragtime should take its place among the higher art forms of music, such as opera and ballet. He wrote a ragtime ballet called *The Ragtime Dance* and spent many years writing the ragtime operas *A Guest of Honor* and *Treemonisha.* Unfortunately, none of these efforts received much attention in his lifetime.

In 1893, Joplin attended The World Columbian Exposition in Chicago. This was also called The Chicago World Fair. It was there that Joplin first saw musicians from Africa perform their work. He was surprised to learn that many people respected their music. White audiences seemed to **appreciate** these black musicians. Unfortunately, they were not allowed to play on the main stage with white musicians. Still, Joplin felt encouraged. He hoped that someday, the ragtime music he loved would receive the same respect.

The Good Days

Around 1894, Joplin moved back to Sedalia, Missouri. Later that year, he left to tour with the Texas Medley Quartette. At this time, the "quartette" had eight members and was considered a double quartette. For the first time, two of his songs were published on sheet music. Joplin wrote both the words and the music for the songs. The songs were not ragtime, but similar to other popular tunes of the day.

Joplin wanted to have more music published. For many years, he had memorized the music he composed, so he didn't always write it down. He needed to learn more about **translating** the notes he played onto sheet music. That way other musicians could play it, too. In 1897, he decided to study music at George R. Smith College. It was a school in Sedalia for black students. In the evenings, Joplin played music for the public. During the day, he attended classes. He quickly grew skilled at writing music.

Sedalia was a **segregated** town, as were most parts of the Midwest at the time. Most blacks lived in a separate part of town. They could not go to the theaters, schools, and other public places where white people went. As a result, they had their own bands, churches, clubs, and schools. Both black and white people enjoyed music, however. Joplin joined a popular band of black musicians called the Queen City Cornet Band. They played for white audiences and were asked to perform in parades and at concerts. Later, Joplin formed several of his own bands.

©Missouri Historical Society

JOPLIN MOVED BACK TO SEDALIA IN 1894. THERE HE DECIDED
TO ATTEND COLLEGE TO LEARN MORE ABOUT WRITING MUSIC.

Anuj Shrestha

WHILE JOPLIN ATTENDED COLLEGE IN SEDALIA, HE STILL PERFORMED HIS MUSIC IN SALOONS AND AT CONCERTS. HE WAS PLEASED THAT PEOPLE ENJOYED RAGTIME.

Ragtime was becoming more and more popular. Its popularity grew in part because of a dance called "the cakewalk." The high-stepping moves of the cakewalk were a good match with the upbeat ragtime sound. And like ragtime, the cakewalk started in the black community, but it became popular among black and white people.

As ragtime's popularity increased, Joplin soon had his first ragtime sheet music published. Joplin's "Original Rags" was published in 1899. One of his most famous works, "Maple Leaf Rag," was also published in 1899.

Joplin formed a partnership with John Stark, a music publisher. Their relationship lasted for two decades. Stark offered to publish Joplin's "Maple Leaf Rag." He promised to give Joplin one cent for each piece of sheet music sold.

By this time, sheet music usually sold for between 25 and 50 cents. In its first year, "Maple Leaf Rag" sold only 400 copies. Joplin earned just $4. But this deal later made a lot of money for both Joplin and Stark. "Maple Leaf Rag" became so popular that Stark received

thousands of orders. By 1909, it had sold more than 500,000 copies. Joplin received a steady income from "Maple Leaf Rag" throughout his life.

BY 1909, MUSIC LOVERS HAD BOUGHT MORE THAN **500,000** COPIES OF "MAPLE LEAF RAG."

©Missouri Historical Society

ONCE JOPLIN'S SONGS WERE AVAILABLE ON SHEET MUSIC, GROUPS SUCH AS THE POPULAR ST. LOUIS COTTON CLUB BAND BEGAN TO PERFORM THEM. THEY HAD AUDIENCES TAPPING THEIR TOES AND CLAPPING THEIR HANDS. THEY ALSO BROUGHT MORE ATTENTION TO AFRICAN AMERICAN MUSIC.

THIS SHEET MUSIC SHOWS DANCERS DOING THE CAKEWALK. LIKE RAGTIME, THE CAKEWALK GOT ITS START IN THE AFRICAN AMERICAN COMMUNITY.

Joplin became known as "The King of Ragtime Writers," which was later shortened to "The King of Ragtime." He often played at the Maple Leaf Club in Sedalia. His fans there called him "The Entertainer." He later used this title as the name for what was to become one of his most famous rags.

Joplin's music was very popular, and his sheet music was in high demand. Around 1900, Joplin married Belle Hayden, the widow of one of his friends. In 1901, Joplin and his wife moved to St. Louis. He began to focus more on composing and less on performing. It was at this time that Joplin began writing a ballet called *The Ragtime Dance.* Getting Stark to publish the work was difficult for Joplin. Stark did not believe it would make money.

In 1902, Stark finally gave in and published the ballet. Just as he had thought, most people didn't like it. But Joplin's ragtime sheet music continued to sell successfully.

During the time that Joplin stopped performing so often, ragtime began to change. The newer rags were flashier, with faster tempos. Joplin did not like this new form of ragtime. The message, "Not to be played fast," appeared on his sheet music. He wanted ragtime to be taken seriously. The faster style seemed to just be a passing craze.

Joplin continued to write slower, more serious ragtime music. He also began working on a ragtime opera called *A Guest of Honor.* His focus on this new project took a toll on his marriage. His wife felt that he did not pay enough attention to her. When she discovered that they were expecting a baby, they were both happy. They hoped it would help their marriage. Unfortunately, the baby was born ill and died after only a few months. Soon after, the couple separated. Joplin decided to take *A Guest of Honor* on tour.

The opera did not do well. Some members of the cast left the show after just one month. The **company** soon broke up. Joplin then moved to Chicago for a few months.

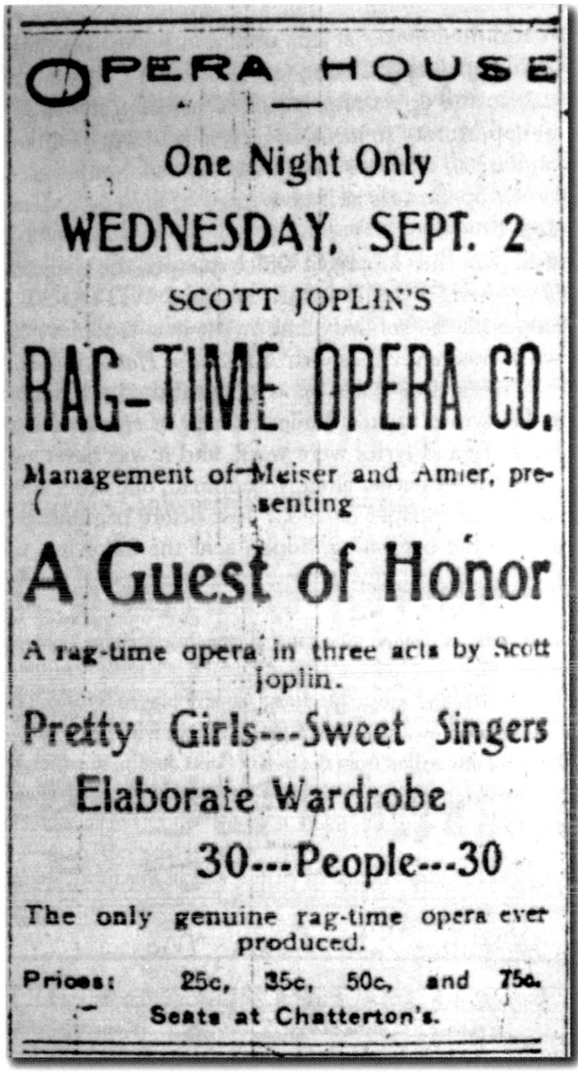
OPERA HOUSE

One Night Only

WEDNESDAY, SEPT. 2

SCOTT JOPLIN'S

RAG-TIME OPERA CO.

Management of Meiser and Amier, presenting

A Guest of Honor

A rag-time opera in three acts by Scott Joplin.

Pretty Girls---Sweet Singers

Elaborate Wardrobe

30---People---30

The only genuine rag-time opera ever produced.

Prices: 25c, 35c, 50c, and 75c.

Seats at Chatterton's.

Library of Congress

THIS ADVERTISEMENT CALLED *A GUEST OF HONOR* "THE ONLY GENUINE RAG-TIME OPERA EVER PRODUCED." PRICES FOR TICKETS TO THE SHOW RANGED FROM 25 TO 75 CENTS.

RAGTIME IS DIFFICULT MUSIC TO PLAY. JOPLIN WROTE *THE SCHOOL OF RAGTIME* TO TEACH MUSICIANS HOW TO PLAY RAGTIME MUSIC WELL.

In 1904, Joplin visited relatives in Arkansas. There he met and married his second wife, Freddie Alexander. She moved with him to Sedalia. Shortly after the marriage, Freddie caught a bad cold that turned into a serious illness. She was never able to recover and died only 10 weeks after their marriage. Joplin was heartbroken. He left Sedalia, never to return.

Joplin traveled around the Midwest, spending most of his time in St. Louis. He continued to publish ragtime music. He moved to Chicago in early 1907 and then went on to New York. John Stark had moved his music-publishing company there a few years earlier. The two men renewed their partnership.

Soon, Joplin had many new pieces of music published. He began playing in concerts and toured the East Coast. During this time, he wrote a book titled

The School of Ragtime. Published in 1908, this book taught musicians the right way to play ragtime. Joplin wanted musicians to work at playing ragtime well. He thought this was better than just making the music easier to play.

While in New York, Joplin met and married his third wife, Lottie Stokes. Lottie was supportive of his career. Joplin seemed to be happy once again.

JOPLIN WORKED WITH MUSIC PUBLISHER JOHN STARK FOR MORE THAN **20** YEARS. TOGETHER THEY PUBLISHED JOPLIN'S MOST POPULAR PIECES.

Library of Congress

The Final Years

As Scott Joplin grew older, "serious" musicians began to **criticize** ragtime. Newspaper articles said that if young people were listening to ragtime, they would never learn about "good" music. These people believed that classical music was the most important kind. Many years later, people would say the same things about both rock-and-roll and rap music.

Some people thought that criticizing ragtime was a kind of **racism.** Although ragtime started in the black community, it had become popular with many whites — especially young people. Many Americans did not want whites and blacks to enjoy the same things or to go to the same places. Most white people still believed that blacks and whites should be segregated.

Joplin believed that if he could create serious ragtime music, people would begin to appreciate it. He began to work on his second opera, *Treemonisha* (tree-moh-NEE-shuh). Because he and his wife did not have much money, he continued to tour occasionally. He also published ragtime sheet music from time to time. For several years, however, most of his energy went into writing *Treemonisha.*

The main character of the opera is an educated black woman named Treemonisha. She helps her people overcome **ignorance** and **superstition.** As the opera begins, the audience learns about Treemonisha's life. As a baby, she was found under a tree by a married couple, Monisha and Ned, who lived in Arkansas. They called her Treemonisha and raised her as their own. When Treemonisha was seven years old, her parents asked a white woman to teach her how to read and write. Most blacks at this time did not have these skills.

©Bettmann/CORBIS

JOPLIN TRIED TO CREATE MORE "SERIOUS"
RAGTIME MUSIC WHEN HE WROTE *TREEMONISHA.*
HE HOPED TO GAIN MORE RESPECT FOR HIS
WORK AND FOR RAGTIME MUSIC.

The opera begins when Treemonisha is 18 years old. Her community is filled with former slaves who need help. They often are tricked by people selling "lucky" rabbits' feet, powders, and potions that are supposed to bring good luck. Because she has been educated, Treemonisha knows that these items will not really bring luck. The people begin to understand that they need a leader. They ask her to guide them.

The story of *Treemonisha* was important to Joplin, who believed that education was the key to black people's success. He put all of his energy into writing the opera and finished it in 1911. He spent the next several years trying to get it published but did not have much success. He finally gave up and published it himself with borrowed money. Although *Treemonisha* got a good **review,** Joplin still could not get support to produce the play.

Finally, in 1915, Joplin was able to put on one performance of the opera at a theater in Harlem, New York. There was not enough money for the actors to have costumes. There was no scenery on the stage. He could not afford a full orchestra. Most of the people in the audience were Joplin's friends. Joplin was hurt that the opera was not a success. He never fully got over this failure. He became sad and began to act strangely.

Joplin began to forget how to play some of his music. He sometimes thought that people were trying to steal his work. By late 1916, he had a hard time paying attention. In early 1917, Joplin was sent to the hospital. He could not move parts of his body, and he did not recognize his visitors.

On April 1, 1917, Joplin died at the age of 49. A serious disease had destroyed his mind and body. At the time he died, ragtime was losing its popularity. People were becoming interested in a new kind of music called jazz.

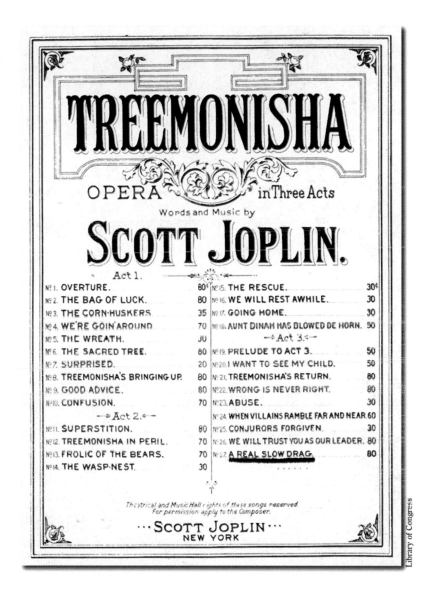

SCOTT JOPLIN COULD NOT FIND SOMEONE TO PUBLISH THE SHEET MUSIC FOR *TREEMONISHA,* SO HE PUBLISHED IT HIMSELF. *TREEMONISHA* CONTAINS SOME OF JOPLIN'S MOST BEAUTIFUL MUSIC. UNFORTUNATELY, JOPLIN NEVER SAW THE OPERA PERFORMED THE WAY HE WANTED.

Gone but Not Forgotten

Joplin once said that people would appreciate his music more after he died. He was right. Beginning in the mid-1940s and 1950s, there was new interest in ragtime and in Joplin. Until her death in 1953, Lottie Joplin tried to keep her husband's music alive. Some articles and books were written about him in the 1950s. In the 1960s, the interest continued to grow.

In January 1972, *Treemonisha* was performed in Atlanta, Georgia, at the Memorial Arts Center. It was part of a weeklong African American Music Workshop at Morehouse College. Newspaper articles reported that the audience enjoyed the performance.

In the 1970s, a true **revival** began. A composer named Marvin Hamlisch selected some of Joplin's music for use in a movie called *The Sting*. The movie starred two famous actors named Paul Newman and Robert Redford. It won an Academy Award for "best picture" of 1972. This award is very important in the movie industry. The title song — Joplin's "The Entertainer" rag — also won an Academy Award. "The Entertainer" was renamed "The Sting" for the movie.

After the movie's success, there was a huge interest in both ragtime and Scott Joplin. Musicians recorded his work. More than 60 years after it was written, *Treemonisha* was produced in New York City. In 1975, the play opened to a full audience on Broadway, the famous part of New York City where plays are performed.

VISITORS TO SEA WORLD IN JOPLIN'S HOME
STATE OF TEXAS STOP TO ADMIRE A STATUE
OF HIM. JOPLIN'S MUSIC HAS RECEIVED MORE
APPRECIATION IN RECENT YEARS.

©Bettmann/CORBIS

By the time Joplin died in 1917, Americans had turned their attention away from ragtime and toward an exciting new kind of music called jazz. Soon trumpeter Louis Armstrong would be one of the country's favorite musicians.

In 1976, Joplin's memory was honored with a **prestigious** award, the Pulitzer Prize. It was awarded for *Treemonisha* and for his contribution to American music. Surely Joplin would have been proud of this great honor.

Today music lovers finally recognize *Treemonisha* as a work of art. In the summer of 2000, the Opera Theater of St. Louis presented the opera on the opening night of its 25th anniversary season. This was special because Joplin lived in St. Louis for so many years. The director of the opera noted that things were very different when Joplin wrote *Treemonisha*. African Americans rarely were portrayed as intelligent people in plays and other works of the day. But Joplin wanted to show that black people could be smart, educated, and good. The director said that portraying "a young, black, educated woman as an inspiring leader shows incredible sensitivity on Joplin's part." Joplin would undoubtedly be very happy that people are taking seriously the most important music he ever wrote.

A POPULAR MOVIE IN THE **1970**s CALLED *THE STING* BROUGHT NEW ATTENTION TO THE MUSIC OF SCOTT JOPLIN. "THE ENTERTAINER" EVEN WON AN ACADEMY AWARD FOR BEST SONG IN A MOVIE.

Today, there are several ragtime clubs. The members play the music and hold ragtime festivals. These festivals are held all over the United States and in other countries each year. The Scott Joplin Ragtime Festival, held in Sedalia, Missouri, is especially important because of the time that Joplin spent there.

In 1983, the United States Postal Service honored Scott Joplin on a 20-cent stamp in its Black Heritage collection. In 1998 and 1999, a production of a musical play called *Ragtime* appeared on Broadway. It was called one of the last great musicals of the century and won numerous awards.

Although Scott Joplin did not live to see it, he knew that people would truly appreciate his music one day. No matter what happened, he kept sight of his goals. Joplin composed quality music — even when others did not understand or appreciate it. Thanks to Joplin, ragtime will forever be a meaningful part of music history.

©Kelly-Mooney Photography/CORBIS

ACTORS FROM THE BROADWAY PLAY *RAGTIME* POSE FOR A PHOTOGRAPH IN NEW YORK CITY. THIS MUSICAL CREATED NEW INTEREST IN JOPLIN'S MUSIC.

Timeline

1868   Scott Joplin is born in east Texas on November 24.

1881 or 1882   Joplin's mother buys him his first piano.

1888 or 1899   Joplin leaves Texarkana, Arkansas, to pursue a career in music, settling briefly in Sedalia, Missouri.

1890   Joplin moves to St. Louis, Missouri, and plays at the Silver Dollar Saloon.

1893   Joplin attends the World Columbian Exposition (the Chicago World Fair) in Chicago, Illinois.

1894   Joplin returns to Sedalia. Later in the year, he tours with the Texas Medley Quartette.

1895   Joplin's first two songs are published. They are called "Please Say You Will" and "A Picture of Her Face." They are not ragtime music.

1897   Joplin enters George Smith College.

1899   Joplin has his first ragtime music, "Original Rags," published.

1899   "Maple Leaf Rag," one of Joplin's most famous songs, is published.

1900   Joplin marries Belle Hayden.

1901   Joplin and his wife move to St. Louis, in part to work more closely with his publisher, John Stark. He signs a five-year contract with Stark.

1902   Joplin's "The Entertainer" is published. *The Ragtime Dance,* a ballet, is also published but is not successful.

1903   Joplin completes his first opera, *A Guest of Honor.*

1904   Joplin meets and marries Freddie Alexander in Arkansas. They return to Sedalia. Freddie Joplin dies within 10 weeks of their marriage.

Joplin leaves Sedalia, never to return. He will spend most of the next two years in St. Louis.

1907   Joplin moves to Chicago and then to New York. He marries his third wife, Lottie Stokes.

1908   Joplin's book, *The School of Ragtime,* is published. It teaches musicians how to play ragtime correctly.

1911   *Treemonisha* is published.

1915   *Treemonisha* is performed in New York.

1917   On April 1, Scott Joplin dies at age 49 in New York City.

1953   Lottie Joplin, Scott's wife, dies. Until that time, she has attempted to keep her husband's music alive.

1974   *The Sting* wins an Academy Award for best picture.

1975   *Treemonisha* is performed on Broadway.

1976   Joplin's memory is honored with the Pulitzer Prize for music.

1983   The United States Postal Service honors Joplin on a 20-cent stamp.

1998   A musical play called *Ragtime* opens on Broadway. It receives many awards.

Glossary

appreciate
(uh-PREE-she-ayt)
When people appreciate something, they recognize its value. Joplin wanted people to appreciate ragtime music.

aspiring
(uh-SPYR-ing)
A person who is aspiring hopes to succeed at something. An aspiring musician hopes to become skilled at playing music.

classical music
(KLAS-ih-kull MEW-zik)
Classical music is a kind of music that originated in Europe and is often played by an orchestra or by smaller groups of musicians. J. C. Johnson taught Scott Joplin about European classical music.

company
(KUM-puh-nee)
In the theater world, a company is a group of people who perform together in a play or opera. The company that performed *A Guest of Honor* broke up quickly.

compose
(kum-POHZ)
If people compose music, they invent the tune and usually write the notes down so it can be played again. Scott Joplin could compose music at a young age.

criticize
(KRIT-uh-syz)
If people criticize something, they find fault with it. Some people criticized ragtime because they believed it was not proper music.

freeborn
(FREE-born)
If an African American was freeborn during the time of slavery, he or she was not born a slave. Joplin's mother, Florence Givens, was freeborn.

ignorance
(IG-nur-untz)
Ignorance is a lack of knowledge or education. The main character of *Treemonisha* helped people overcome ignorance.

instrumental
(in-struh-MEN-tul)
Instrumental music is written only for instruments, without lyrics for people to sing. Some ragtime music was instrumental.

lyrics
(LEER-iks)
Lyrics are the words to a song. Some ragtime music has lyrics.

melodious
(muh-LOW-dee-us)
If something is melodious, it has a pleasing melody or sound. Scott Joplin played melodious tunes with an upbeat tempo.

opera
(AH-per-eh)
An opera is a play set to music in which the actors and actresses sing their parts. Joplin wrote ragtime operas, including *A Guest of Honor* and *Treemonisha*.

prestigious
(preh-STEEJ-us)
If something is prestigious, it is considered valuable. After he died, Scott Joplin's memory was honored with the prestigious Pulitzer Prize.

quartette
(kwor-TET)
A quartette is a musical group with four members. Although a quartette usually has four members, the Texas Medley Quartette had five members.

Glossary

racism
(RAY-sih-zim)
Racism is a negative feeling or opinion about people because of their race. Racism can be committed by individuals, large groups, or even governments.

ragtime
(RAG-tym)
Ragtime is a type of music made popular in the late 19th century. Ragtime music has a strong melody combined with a regular beat.

review
(ree-VEW)
A review gives comments and opinions (usually in a newspaper or magazine or on television) about something, such as a play, movie, concert, or book. *Treemonisha* got a good review in a magazine.

revival
(ree-VY-vul)
A revival is when something becomes popular again. There was a revival of ragtime's popularity in the 1970s.

saloons
(suh-LOONZ)
Saloons are places where alcoholic drinks are sold and drunk. Sometimes music is played at saloons.

segregated
(SEH-grih-gay-ted)
If something is segregated, it cannot be used equally by all people. Many places in the United States were once segregated, so African Americans either could not enter or were separated from white people.

sharecroppers
(SHAIR-krop-erz)
Sharecroppers are farmers who work on another person's land. The landowner gives the farmers seed, tools, stock, living quarters, and food. The farmer receives part of the crop as payment. Scott Joplin's parents were sharecroppers.

superstition
(su-pur-STISH-un)
Superstition is a belief that is based on fear or hope, not on reason or fact. Believing that a rabbit's foot will bring luck is a superstition.

tempo
(TEM-poh)
Tempo is the speed at which music is played. Scott Joplin's music had an upbeat tempo, but it was not played as fast as ragtime music by other composers.

translating
(TRAN-slayt-ing)
In music, translating means to write music down on paper in the form of notes. Translating music allows other people to play it.

vulgar
(VUL-gur)
If something is vulgar, it is considered rude or improper. The lyrics to some ragtime songs were vulgar.

Index

Further Information

Books

Igus, Toyomi, and Michelle Wood. *I See Rhythm.* San Francisco: Children's Book Press, 1998.

Otfinoski, Steven. *Scott Joplin: A Life of Ragtime.* New York: Grolier Publishing, 1995.

Silverman, Jerry. *Just Listen to This Song I'm Singing: African-American History Through Song.* Brookfield, CT: Millbrook Press, 1996.

Silverman, Jerry. *Ragtime Song and Dance* (Traditional Black Music). Philadelphia: Chelsea House, 1995.

Stanley, Leotha. *Be a Friend. The Story of African American Music in Song, Words, and Pictures.* Madison, WI: Zino Press Children's Books, 1995.

Web Sites

Listen to rags by Joplin and find links to other Web sites about Joplin and ragtime music:
http://www.ddc.com/~decoy/sjop.htm
http://members.tripod.com/~perfessorbill/pbmidi.htm

Read biographies about Scott Joplin:
http://www.incwell.com/Biographies/Joplin.html
http://www.geocities.com/BourbonStreet/Bayou/9694/

Visit the Archives of African American Music and Culture:
http://www.indiana.edu/~aaamc/

Missouri State Parks — Scott Joplin Historic Site:
http://www.mostateparks.com/scottjoplin.htm

Learn about African American classical musicians:
http://ezinfo.ucs.indiana.edu/~afamarch/home.html

Visit the Scott Joplin International Ragtime Foundation:
http://www.scottjoplin.org/

Dowload sheet music for Scott Joplin's compositions:
http://www.virtualsheetmusic.com/engines/Joplin/Joplin.html

Read the words to *Treemonisha:*
http://www.io.com/~cortese/joplin/libretto.html